# SILENT POETRY

## *Work and Leisure in Fine Art*

by Andrea Stowe

# NOTE TO PARENTS

Art is magic. It can take us to the places we dream of, and shape our minds like no other art form can. The artist has the power to capture a single moment and immortalize it for eternity. When we look at his work, we are transported back in time to view the world through his eyes. No textbook can describe

Renaissance Europe as vividly as Bruegel can paint it.

The paintings in this book span the timeline from Ancient China to the late 19th century. They are drawn from various artistic movements, cultures, and countries, and will take you and your young artists on an adventure to far off times and places.

Best of all, you can begin this journey in only a few minutes at a time. Start by looking at a painting in this book once or twice a week during your school day or bedtime routine. Take five to ten minutes to look at a painting together and talk through the provided discussion questions. Additional biographical information on each artist is provided at the end of the book.

For a more multi-sensory experience, use the playlist (located at the back of the book on page 26) and listen to musical selections that historically correspond with the different art movements.

We are visual and creative beings, and beautiful paintings have the power to educate us in a way that mere words cannot. May this book encourage you to embrace fine art just a little bit more!

*Andrea Stowe*

*"Painting is silent poetry, and poetry is a painting that speaks."*
*~Simonides of Ceos*

# HOW TO USE THIS BOOK

### Look*

Spend 2-3 minutes of silent, focused time just looking at the painting. Don't worry about the questions yet, just enjoy the beauty of the work, notice what you find interesting or strange, and immerse yourself in the world of the painting.

*For classroom settings, a link to the paintings as Google Slides can be found at the back of the book.

### Listen

While looking at the painting, consider putting on some music to enhance the experience. In the back of this book you will find a link to a playlist designed to compliment each painting in the book. They correspond to the historical and artistic periods of each work of art and are organized in the same order.

### Discuss

When you have finished looking at the painting, use the provided questions to discuss it with your children or students. Encourage them to engage in discussion and refrain from yes or no answers. When you have finished discussing the questions in the book, ask if anything in the painting stood out to them as especially beautiful, interesting, confusing, or funny.

### Dig Deeper

After discussing the painting and your children's impressions of it, share some of the additional information about the artist and his historical period provided in the back of the book. You can adapt this depending on the age and interest of your child, or simply enjoy it yourself.

# TUNING THE ZITHER
## *Ancient China*

## *Discussion Questions*

✱ Can you find two trees?

✱ What do you think these ladies are doing?

✱ Do their clothes look like your clothes?

✱ If you could spend the afternoon with these ladies, what would you talk about?

## *Did you know ....*

A zither is a flat wooden instrument with many strings stretched across it, like a guitar.

**Tang Dynasty**
**(618-907)**

# Agricultural Labours
## *Middle Ages*

## *Discussion Questions*

✱ Can you find the family having breakfast?

✱ What do you think is in the boy's basket?

✱ How is this scene different from your neighborhood?

✱ Which of of these jobs would you like to try?

## *Did you know?*

No one knows who painted this
picture. It's a mystery!

*Medieval Art
1066-1485*

# Children's Games
## *Renaissance*

# *Questions*

✳ Can you find someone doing a handstand?

✳ What sounds do you think you would hear in this village?

✳ What games do you like to play outside with your friends?

✳ How would you feel if you were suddenly a part of this painting?

**Pieter Bruegel
d. 1569**

*Oil on Panel
46.5"x63"
Kunsthistorisches Museum*

## *Did you know …*

Both of Pieter Bruegel's sons
became artists like their
father.

# The Rainbow Landscape
## *Dutch Baroque*

## *Questions*

✻ Can you find three red shirts?

✻ What do you think the ladies are talking about?

✻ Have you ever seen a rainbow like the one in this painting?

✻ What would you do if you met a herd of cows in the road?

**Peter Paul Rubens**
**1577-1640**

*Oil on Panel*
*53.3"x92.5"*
**The Wallace Collection**

## *Did you know …*

Peter Paul Rubens painted one of the most expensive paintings in any museum today. It sold for $76,000,000!

# The Swing
## *Rococo*

## *Questions*

✳ Can you find six faces?

✳ Where do you think the ladies shoe will land?

✳ Do you have a swing at home?

✳ What do you think it's like to wear a clothes like that?

**Jean-Honore Fragonard
(1732-1806)**

*Oil on Canvas
31.8" × 25.1"
The Wallace Collection*

## *Did you know …*

One of Jean-Honore Fragonard's favorite models was his daughter, Rosalie.

# Home in the Woods
## *Romanticism*

## *Questions*

✻ Can you find the family's laundry hanging out to dry?

✻ Do you think it is morning or evening in this painting? Can you tell me why?

✻ Have you ever caught a fish before?

✻ How would you feel if your home was in the woods?

### *Thomas Cole (1801-1848)*

*Oil on Canvas*
*52.5" × 74.5"*
*Reynolds House, Museum of Art*

## *Did you know …*

One of the highest mountain peaks in New York is named after Thomas Cole!

# The Serenade
## *Academic Classicism*

## *Questions*

✳ Can you find a bright red earring?

✳ Do you think the ladies are enjoying the music? What makes you say that?

✳ Can you play an instrument?

✳ Would you like to visit this fishing village?

## *Did you know …*

This artist could sign his name five different ways!
- *Eugen Blaas*
- *Eugene de Blaas*
- *Eugene de Blas*
- *Eugenio von Blaas*
- *Eugene Von Blass*

**Eugene De Blaas
(1843-1931)**

**Oil on Canvas
37.5"x44"
Private collection
Peter Guarisco**

# October

*Naturalism*

## *Questions*

✻ Can you find five people working?

✻ Can you tell me what these people are doing?

✻ What is your favorite way to cook and eat potatoes?

✻ How would you like to work in a field like this?

✻

## *Did you know …*

Jules Bastien-Lepage grew up in a small French town where his family grew grapes and fruit trees.

**Jules Bastien-Lepage
(1848-1884)**

*Oil on Canvas
74.1"x 77.3"
National Gallery of Victoria*

# The Boating Party
## *Impressionism*

## *Questions*

* Can you find the houses on shore?

* Does the baby look like she's having fun? What makes you say that?

* Have you ever ridden in a boat? Can you tell me about it?

* How would you feel if you were in this boat and it started to rain?

**Mary Cassat (1844-1926)**

**Oil on Canvas 37.5"x 46.2" National Gallery of Art**

## *Did you know …*

Mary Cassat was the only American artist whose work was exhibited with the great French Impressionists.

# First Steps
## *Post-Impressionism*

## *Questions*

✶ Can you find some red flowers?

✶ Can you tell me what is happening in this picture?

✶ Does this look like your back yard?

✶ Would you like to work in this garden?

## *Did you know …*

Vincent van Gogh painted over
900 paintings in only ten years! 43
of them were self-portraits.

**Vincent van Gogh
(1853-1890)**

*Oil on Canvas
28.5"x 35.8"
Metropolitan Museum of Art*

# Further Information

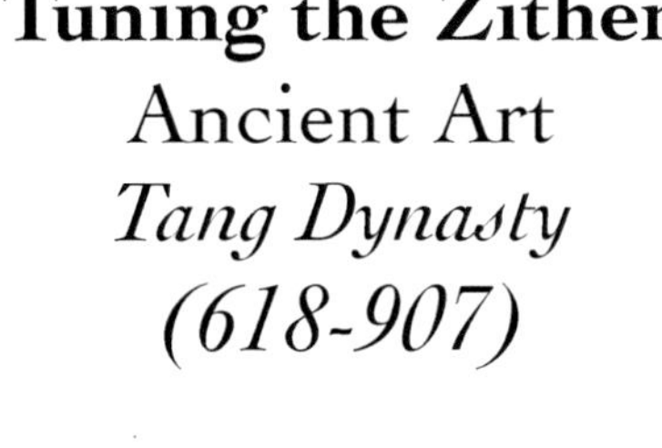

## Tuning the Zither
### Ancient Art
*Tang Dynasty*
*(618-907)*

This painting was created in Ancient China during the Tang Dynasty. Music was very important to the Chinese people and the Tang Dynasty they welcomed new ideas and instruments from other countries and cultures. The people made music for pleasure and entertainment and even developed methods for writing down musical scores for many instruments! Because music was such an important part of the culture, many paintings from this period depict people making music together.

## Agricultural Labours
### Medieval Art
*Artist Unknown*
*1066-1485*

This picture comes from a Medieval book. It was published before the invention of the printing press when all books were written and illustrated by hand. These books were works of art in themselves and included elaborate decorations and borders around the letters and pages. The artists used complicated methods to create different colored paints made of egg whites and crushed colored stones or earth. They even used very thin pieces of gold in their paintings to make them glow and sparkle

## Children's Games
### Rennaisance
*Pieter Bruegel*
*d. 1569*

Pieter Bruegel was born in the Netherlands and was an important figure in the formation of Dutch Renaissance art. Before Bruegel most artists painted primarily religious scenes, but he focused on painting the beautiful landscapes that surrounded him and the people who lived in them. He did paint religious scenes as well, but set them in his own world. For example, in his painting of the Holy Family entering Bethlehem, the town appears as a Renaissance peasant village. Pieter Bruegel married the

## The Rainbow Landscape
### Dutch Baroque
*Peter Paul Rubens*
*(1577-1640)*

Peter Paul Rubens was a Catholic artist from Germany. He painted in the Baroque style which employs lots of elaborate detail and ornamentation. He particularly enjoyed painting religious and mythological subjects and was known for making ordinary things look incredibly beautiful and idealized. He even managed to make Philip II of Spain look heroic in his famous painting of him on horseback! In addition to art, Rubens also loved history and collected coins, sculptures, and writings of Ancient

## The Swing
### Jean-Honore Fragonard
*Rococo*
### (1732-1806)

Fragonard was a French artist of the Rococo movement. Art from this era  is known for being extremely detailed and emphasizing human beauty. It is usually bright, elegant, and highly-ornamented. Fragonard was born to a working class family and was first apprenticed to a lawyer. This man told Fragonard's family that he had a talent for art and should be indulged in his interest. His family therefore sent him to study under Francois Boucher and eventually he went to art college. He copied many Roman Baroque paintings and also focused on landscapes for a time. Finally he began painting many elaborate outdoor party scenes including this one. During his life, Fragonard produced an over 550 paintings in addition to several

## Home in the Woods
### Thomas Cole
*Romanticism*
### (1801-1848)

Thomas Cole was an English artist who moved to the United States when he was seventeen. As an artist, he was primarily self-taught. He studied great artists of the past and used them as his inspiration. Cole began working as a portrait painter and eventually chose to spend most of his time painting landscapes. He was a Romantic artist which means that he loved nature and used his art to make statements against industrialism. Cole married Maria Bartow and they moved to the Catskills in New York. The Coles had five children and one of them grew up to become an artist like her father.

## The Serenade
### Eugene de Blaas
*Academic Classicism*
### (1843-1931)

Eugene de Blaas was born in Rome, to Austrian parents. His father was an artist and taught both Eugene and his brother to paint. As a young adult Eugene moved to Venice where he enjoyed painting scenes from everyday life. Rich people liked his work , especially because he smoothed over all the dirt and hard work of the commoners and made then look beautiful and cheerful! He also painted some portraits and religious art, but his best loved and admired works were his paintings of normal people doing everyday things.

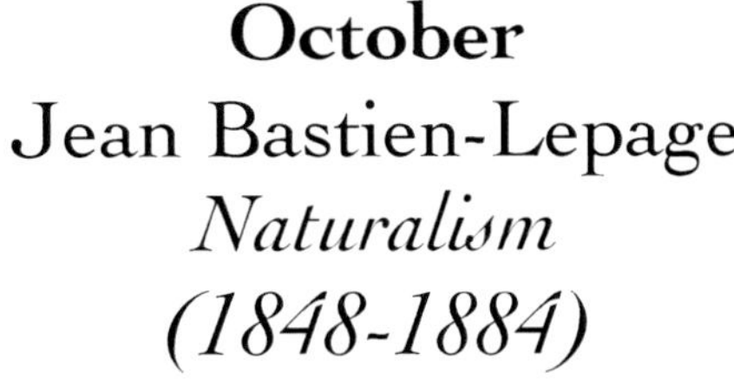

## October
### Jean Bastien-Lepage
*Naturalism*
*(1848-1884)*

Jean Bastien-Lepage was a French Naturalist painter who focused primarily on rural outdoor scenes. As every successful artist must, he exhibited at the Salon of Paris. One of his most famous paintings is a portrait of Joan of Arc as a young French peasant girl. His paintings incredibly realistic and include very fine details. The advent of photography provoked two major art movements: Impressionism and Naturalism. Impressionism proved that painting was still a valuable artistic medium because it could express things that photography could not, such as emotional perceptions of a scene or moving light and shadows. In contrast, Naturalism used the technology photography offered to create even more realistic and detailed paintings. This was the first time that artists painted from photos instead of from life.

## The Boating Party
### Impressionism
*Mary Cassat*
*(1844-1926)*

Mary Cassat was and Impressionist painter born in Pennsylvania in 1844. She was the daughter of a banker and was educated by a private art tutor while traveling throughout Europe. When she grew older Cassat moved to Paris to study with the great Impressionists. Edgar Degas himself saw her talent and invited her to exhibit her paintings with and officially join the French Impressionists. She also went through a period of painting Japanese inspired art, but her most beloved works are those that depict the beauty of women and children doing every day things.

## First Steps
### Post-Impressionism
*Vincent van Gogh*
*(1853-1890)*

Vincent Van Gogh was born in the Netherlands in 1853. Several of his uncles were art dealers and he was apprenticed to one of them at sixteen. During his training there Vincent came to love art and painting, but ultimately dreamed of becoming a missionary and sharing hope with poor coal-miners in Belgium. His passionate approach to preaching, however, intimidated the villagers and they turned him away. Vincent then moved to France to learn more about the Impressionist movement there. He began including bright, bold colors in his works to make them more appealing. Vincent never believed that he was a brilliant artist, but he was certainly a passionate one. After many years of struggling to support himself with his art, Vincent finally died in Auvers, France under mysterious circumstances. Shortly after his death, however, his sister-in-law began working to preserve his art and share it with the public. It is thanks to her that we can still enjoy so much of Vincent's artwork.

# Additional Resources

Musical Accompaniments

Google Slides for Classroom